DATE DUE			
OCT 20 1987			
NOV 2 1988			
OCT 1 7 1990			
NOV 06 1995			
NOV 20 1996			
NOV 1 0 1997			
MAY 1 2 1998			
JAN 1 4 1999			
MAY 1 4 2004			

HIGHSMITH 45-220

Sea Babies

Sea Babies
New Life in the Ocean

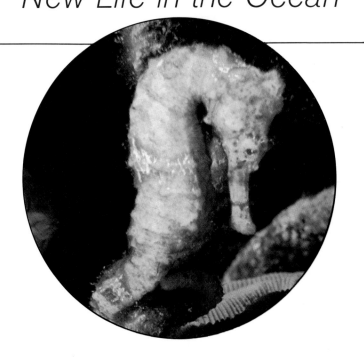

by Jean H. Sibbald

Dillon Press, Inc.   Minneapolis, Minnesota 55415

To Julie and Brett

Library of Congress Cataloging in Publication Data

Sibbald, Jean H.
  Sea babies : new life in the ocean.

  Bibliography: p.
  Includes index.
  Summary: Describes the ways in which various sea creatures give birth to their young, examining such types as beach
babies, river babies, and marine mammal babies and following them as they grow to adulthood.
  1. Marine fauna—Development—Juvenile literature.
2. Marine fauna—Infancy—Juvenile literature. [1. Marine animals—Infancy] I. Title.
QL122.2.S57 1986   591.1'6'09162   85-7039
ISBN 0-87518-305-0

Dillon Press, Inc., 242 Portland Avenue South
Minneapolis, Minnesota 55415

Printed in the United States of America
2 3 4 5 6 7 8 9 10 94 93 92 91 90 89 88 87

Contents

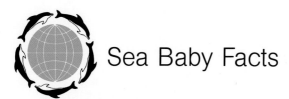 Sea Baby Facts

Size of the Ocean:
  140,000,000 square miles (361,000,000 square kilometers)—71 percent of the earth's surface

Different Species of Sea Animals:
  About 160,000

Biggest Sea Baby:
  Blue Whale—23 feet (7 meters) long; 5000 pounds (2,273 kilograms) at birth

Eggs Laid at One Time:
  Oyster—100 million
  Tuna—4 to 6 million
  Sunfish—300 million
  Blue Crab—2 million

Basic Foods for Sea Babies:
  Plankton—microscopic plants and animals
  Detritus—decaying bits of plants

Greatest Threats to Sea Babies:
  Hungry sea animals
  Water pollution
  Destruction of nursery areas

 Introduction

The world's strangest babies live in the sea. Some sea babies are too tiny to see, while others are larger than a car. There are babies that grow in the mouths of their fathers, while many others never see their parents at all. A few begin life on dry land before moving to the sea. Some grow in **egg*** cases shaped like small collars or miniature purses. Others look nothing at all like their parents and must change shape many times before becoming adults.

Sea babies may be strange, but like all babies, they are important. Without babies, no animal **species** could survive. There must be enough babies surviving to adulthood to replace the adults that die.

Survival in the sea is a neverending struggle. Baby sea creatures are a major source of food for larger sea animals. Currents and waves toss eggs and babies far away from their homes. Changes in water temperature or the amount of salt also can cause the delicate babies to die. Because of all these dangers, most sea babies do not reach adulthood.

The creatures of the sea have developed a number of ways to insure that enough of their babies survive.

---

*Words in **bold type** are explained in the glossary at the end of this book.

Many of the smaller fish and **shellfish** lay millions of eggs at a time. Others bury eggs, hide them, or enclose them in special cases. Some bear their young alive and carefully protect them until they are old enough to protect themselves. Very few, however, give their young the kind of care provided by land animals.

Land animal babies are familiar to us. We can see them, touch them, and watch them grow. We have puppies and kittens and baby brothers and sisters. We see the eggs of birds and chickens, and later can see and hear the chicks that hatch from them. In zoos we can watch the babies of jungle animals, as well as other babies from faraway places around the world.

Even when land animal babies do not look at all like their parents, we can learn to recognize which baby belongs to which adult. We can find caterpillars that will become moths and butterflies and tadpoles that will become frogs or toads.

Learning about the babies of sea creatures is more difficult. The waters hide them from our view and separate them from the adults. Very few can be picked up and handled. The tiniest can be seen only through a

*A baby loggerhead sea turtle strug-
gles to reach the safety of the sea.
(Lynn Stone)*

microscope. But since they seldom look like their parents, we still don't know whose baby we are seeing.

Scientists known as marine biologists have spent many years studying sea life. They go into the sea as scuba divers or in special undersea craft. Marine biologists spend hundreds of hours sitting in boats observing larger animals such as whales and seals. They crouch quietly on beaches and watch turtles lay their eggs. When it is time for the eggs to hatch, they return to watch the babies scramble for the safety of the sea. Marine biologists also collect sea creatures and put them in aquariums. If they're lucky, the creatures may **spawn**, or produce fertilized eggs.

The huge **seaquariums**, such as Marineland and Sea World in Florida and California, have helped scientists learn much about sea creatures and their young. In these settings sea animals live and grow much as they do in the open sea. They can be observed through glass panels without being disturbed.

Sea babies are strange. Sea babies are interesting. Sea babies are different from any other babies in the world.

 Millions of Eggs

If every egg laid in the ocean hatched, there would not be enough room in the world for all the babies to grow. Sea creatures are the world's greatest egg layers. In fact, some can lay more than a million tiny eggs at a time.

Oysters and Eggs in the Sea

Make the smallest dot you can with a pencil on a piece of paper. That dot is larger than the egg of an oyster. The head of a straight pin is about the size of a baby crab. Some sea babies are even smaller.

Even fully grown, many sea animals will be no larger than a person's hand, if that large. Yet the sheer number of creatures, if all should survive, would soon crowd out everything else.

Just imagine the numbers! An oyster five inches (thirteen centimeters) long can lay more than 100 million eggs at a time. A tuna fish or a codfish can carry 4 to 6 million eggs, and a sunfish 300 million. A blue crab lays as many as 2 million eggs at a time, and a shrimp that many or more.

When one sea animal lays its eggs, it is surrounded by others doing the same. An oyster bed may have more than half a million female oysters in it. Imagine each one laying more than 100 million eggs at the same time. Even dot-sized, those **trillions** of eggs make the water milky over the oyster bed.

What happens to all the eggs? Many disappear into the mouths of other animals. Eggs and babies in the sea have two major purposes: to replace adults of their species that die, and to serve as food for other kinds of sea creatures.

In order to develop into a baby, an egg must combine with the **sperm** from a male of the same species. The egg is then fertilized. For most of the eggs tossed into the sea in huge numbers, **fertilization** is a matter of chance. The male tosses out huge batches of sperm or **milt** (the sperm of fish) at the same time as the female lays the eggs. Like tiny magnets, the eggs and sperm attract each other. Many will join. Others are separated by waves and tides and drift about until eaten.

Of all the sea babies that begin developing, few

These oyster shells would form just a small part of the many thousands of oysters that live close together in an oyster bed. (Lynn Stone)

reach adulthood. The others are eaten by the many creatures looking for food. Of a million eggs, maybe one will become an adult.

A baby oyster develops within thirty hours after the egg is fertilized. Although the young creature is too tiny to be seen, its two shells have started to grow, and it has tiny eyes and a foot. At this stage it looks nothing like its parents. For the only time in its life, the oyster is free to swim around. Tiny hairs, or **cilia**, surrounding its body serve as paddles to propel it through the water.

The baby's food is the **microscopic plankton** that floats in the sea. Since plankton is made up of both plant and animal life, the young oyster itself is a part of the plankton.

As the oyster's shell grows, the baby becomes heavier. Before long it can no longer float and settles to the bottom to look for a permanent home. Pulling itself along on its tiny foot, the oyster searches for a clean, hard surface. The best spot is on another oyster shell.

Once a likely spot is found, the young oyster **secretes** a drop of gluelike material. It settles its left shell into the drop and is soon cemented in place for life. This pinhead-sized creature is called a **spat**. It has lost its cilia, its eyes, and its foot. Now it is a tiny animal that looks much like the adult oyster.

Thousands of other oysters surround the spat. They are clumped together in beds that may cover wide areas on the bottom of bays and inlets. Thick, rough, gray shells protect the soft animals inside.

The baby oyster may begin life as a male or female. Its sex isn't important because it will soon change. Oysters, and some other sea creatures, make a habit of changing sex. They may change each year or every few weeks. The amount of food and condition of the water probably affect the number of changes, but scientists do not know for sure how and why such changes occur.

Abalones

Abalone shells look like shallow bowls with a row of small holes along one side. In an adult, the holes may be pea-sized or larger. Eggs and sperm spurt out the holes in little puffs, turning the water a cloudy white.

Baby abalones begin as ball-shaped **larvae**, swimming about as the tiny oysters do. Because they are snails, the baby abalones have only a single shell. The shell is twisted into a tiny spiral. Two **tentacles** and a foot develop on the abalone's body, and they will stay with it for life.

After a week or two of swimming and tumbling about in the plankton, a baby abalone begins crawling around on the bottom. Its shell becomes wider and flatter at the open end. By three months of age, it has developed the first hole in its pinhead-sized shell and is beginning to look like an adult.

Clamping its shell against a rock, the young abalone holds on tightly with its foot. To eat, it raises its shell and crawls along the rock surface. Like most shellfish, the abalone will not wander too far from its chosen home.

Fish

Fish roam throughout the sea. A few bear their young alive, but most produce huge numbers of eggs and leave them. The eggs float about in the plankton, looking like miniature **transparent**, or see-through, balloons. Inside, the developing fish **embryo** is curled around the yolk. When it wriggles free of the egg casing, it carries the yolk on its belly. This will be its

Many unusual fish live in the sea. Lionfish use their fins to inject poison that kills the small creatures they feed on. This poison is also their protection from predators. (James Rowan)

The clownfish lives among the tentacles of the sea anemone. The anemone's stinging tentacles kill fish that the clownfish feeds on and protect the clownfish from predators. (Jacki Kilbride/EarthViews)

food for the first few days. The baby fish cannot swim freely until the yolk is all used up. Seaweeds, stones, and corals provide shelter until the fish **fry**, or babies, are ready to swim away.

The fry of many kinds of fish find their way into protected bays or inlets. They will feed and grow for several months before heading back out to sea. While still young, the fry begin to gather in groups called

schools. They travel together from then on, swimming, feeding, and later spawning.

Shrimp

Baby shrimp have many changes to make before they become adults. An adult shrimp carries millions of greenish eggs, which are visible through its transparent shell. Thirteen or fourteen hours after being released into the water, the eggs hatch. At first, the pinpoint-sized shrimp larva looks like a tiny dot with

hairs become eight legs, four on each side of the body.

By paddling rapidly, the tiny shrimp is able to swim for about five seconds. Then it rests on its back for fifteen seconds before beginning to paddle again. The shrimp larva has a long way to swim. Somehow it must make its way from the hatching place to a nursery area as far as 100 miles (160 kilometers) away.

During the three-week trip, the shrimp changes shape between twenty-one and twenty-seven times. Gradually it develops a tail. Then the body begins to show sections, or segments, similar to those of the adult shrimp.

In the daytime the shrimp larva sinks down into

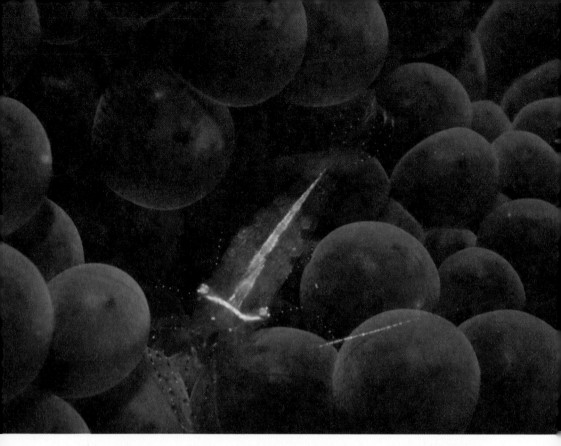

The delicately outlined, mostly transparent body of a shrimp hovers among the anemone near the Fiji Islands of the South Pacific Ocean. (Jacki Kilbride/EarthViews)

the darker, deeper water. At night it rises to the sur-face. The adult shrimp stays near the bottom during the day and buries itself in the mud at night.

By the time the baby shrimp reaches the protected nursery area, it looks like an adult but is much small-er. It feeds and grows for five to seven months before taking the long trip back to the breeding grounds in deep water.

Crabs

A baby crab looks like a strange creature that we might imagine living on some distant planet. A long spike sticks out from the top of its round head. Its huge eyes bulge. Six arms stretch out from the sides of its body, and a long tail hangs below. Fortunately, this creature is so small that it can be seen only through a microscope. A large crab larva, or **zoea**, would be frightening indeed.

A female crab carries her millions of eggs in a spongelike mass on the underside of her body. A male crab left his sperm with the mother several months before. When a crab egg hatches, the tiny zoea swims to the surface of the sea. Since its tough skin will not grow, each time the zoea grows, it casts off its skin.

This shedding, or **molting**, will be done throughout the life of the crab. It can grow in no other way. After five molts, the baby crab begins to look like its parents, except that it still has a long tail. When the next molt is complete, the zoea sinks to the sea floor. Its tail disappears from sight.

The young crab grows rapidly, molting every few days, and then every few weeks. Strong claws develop that give it protection and help it to grab and hold onto

A baby crab goes through many molts before it reaches the size and shape of this adult blue crab. (Allan Roberts)

food. Eyes on little stalks move rapidly from one position to another. As four pairs of legs carry the crab across the sea floor, it looks like an enormous spider. By the time the crab is a year old, it is three to four inches (eight to ten centimeters) across.

Eggs and babies by the millions—that is the way many sea creatures make sure that their species will be a part of the next generation of ocean life.

 Beach Babies

The sea and the land meet at the shore. In some places there are rocks and stones, or sheer cliffs. In other places there are rough grasses and marshes, or long, sandy beaches. It is on the beaches that horseshoe crabs, grunions, and sea turtles begin their lives. These beach babies hatch from eggs protected by a layer of sand that keeps them safe from strong winds and harsh temperatures.

Horseshoe Crabs

More than 350 million years ago, horseshoe crabs were plodding along the bottoms of shallow seas. Before dinosaurs roamed the earth, the horseshoe crab was laying its jellylike eggs. Now, long after dinosaurs have disappeared, the horseshoe still quietly goes about its harmless life. Its brittle, brown, dome-shaped shell looks somewhat like a huge horse's hoof with a tail.

The horseshoe is not really a crab at all. In fact, it

is related to spiders and ticks. Fortunately, neither of those land creatures grows as large as the horseshoe. Just imagine a foot-long spider or tick!

By some means unknown to us, the horseshoe knows when spring tides are highest and picks those times to come ashore. The males hitch a free ride on the tails of the females.

A female horseshoe pulls onto the sand of Atlantic coast beaches, just beyond the edge of the sea. She burrows partially in the sand, buries a clump of jelly-like eggs, and then moves away. For about a month the eggs rest in the damp sand. Each looks like a tiny greenish glass bead with a whitish blob in the middle. The blob soon develops legs and the shell and shape of the horseshoe crab.

When the egg hatches beneath the sand, the horse-shoe is only 1/8-inch (1/3-centimeter) wide. A dozen could fit on a person's thumbnail. The baby's pale body has only a nub of a tail, but otherwise it looks like a miniature adult. A part of the egg yolk is still attached to serve as food until the tiny creature can eat on its own.

On a moonlit night when high tides cover the sand above the nest, the horseshoe hatchlings wriggle and

This young horseshoe crab will soon outgrow its shell, molt, and form a new, larger shell that will allow it to keep growing. (Lynn Stone)

kick and push to the surface of the sand. Waves wash them into the sea where millions of the tiny babies float on the waves.

Soon they settle to the bottom to feed on even smaller creatures. Their tails get longer, and their soft bodies grow, becoming squashed inside the hard shell. Finally, the shell splits around the front rim. Then the horseshoe walks out, much bigger than the shell it has left behind. The new shell hardens around the horse-shoe, which will continue to molt as it grows.

The light tan sheds, or molts, often wash ashore. They look exactly like the real animal, legs and all, but there is nothing inside.

By the time they are three years old, horseshoe crabs are six inches (fifteen centimeters) wide. The female is larger than the male. As horseshoes get older, they grow more slowly and molt less often. Fully grown adults have such permanent shells that other creatures such as barnacles and slipper shells make their homes on them.

Grunions

While horseshoe crabs are busy on the Atlantic coast, California beaches are the scene of one of nature's strangest happenings. Masses of silvery little fish flop out of the water and onto the shore. They are grunions coming to lay their eggs in the sand.

Like the horseshoe crabs, the six- to eight-inch-long (fifteen- to twenty-one-centimeter long) grunions know when the tides are highest. At night, after the peak tide has begun to ebb, the little fish appear. The female digs into the sand with her tail until she is half buried. She makes a little grunting sound, and then drops as many as 3,000 tiny pinkish eggs into the sand. One or more males curl close to her, covering the eggs with their sperm. Once her work is done, the female flops back and forth and bursts out of the sand. All the grunions wriggle back into the sea. The entire process takes just thirty seconds.

Tides will not cover the area for ten or more days, long enough for tiny embryos to grow in the eggs. If you could look inside an egg, you would see two black eyes on a head that seems too big for the long skinny body. The grunion embryo is curled around the yolk food supply.

When seawater returns to the nest, it seeps through the sand and soaks the grunion eggs. Wave motion rolls the grains of sand and shakes the eggs. Within two or three minutes, 1/4-inch-long (2/3-centimeter-long) fry pop from the eggs and wriggle up through the sand. Out into the sea they go on the crashing waves.

Sea Turtles

Sea turtles are the largest of the beach babies, and the only ones that must walk to the sea. Like the horseshoe and grunion, the female loggerhead sea turtle comes ashore just after the peak of the highest tides. In the dark of night she hauls her heavy body out of the sea. Her shell is larger than a car tire, and large flippers serve as legs. Without the support of the water, her heavy body—300 pounds (134 kilograms) or more—moves slowly.

The loggerhead's huge head drags in the sand as she lumbers up the beach. From time to time she stops, lifts her head, and takes a deep, gasping breath. Sea turtles have lungs like land animals. Even in the water they must rise to the surface to breathe.

The female loggerhead moves high up on the beach. Folding her hind flippers into small shovels, she digs a hole more than a foot deep. About 120 eggs are laid in the hole before the turtle carefully fills it with sand. She then brushes a large area around the hole with her flippers to hide the marks of her digging. At last she lumbers back down the beach and into the sea.

The soft, leathery turtle eggs are perfectly round and as big as the round part of a hen's egg. The baby loggerhead grows inside for eight to ten weeks. When ready to hatch, it slashes the egg with a sharp tooth on the tip of its snout. Since all that work exhausts the baby turtle, it spends the next twenty-four hours resting.

Finally the big day arrives. All the babies crawl out of their eggs and struggle to reach the surface. More than a hundred wriggling little bodies are piled on top of each other in the dark hole deep in the sand.

Getting out is a group activity. The baby turtles move together and rest together. The top ones dig at the sand above, and the bottom ones trample it down. At last the top turtles reach the open air. When night comes, they burst out, followed by the entire nest of baby loggerheads. All head straight for the sea, skittering across the sand on their tiny flippers.

Very few, though, will reach the sea. Birds and sand crabs wait to scoop up the tiny creatures. Even the sea is not safe because sharks and other large fish will make a meal of baby loggerheads. Only a few babies from a nest will safely reach the deep water.

A few lucky ones may find a clump of floating seaweed for shelter and a free ride. Safely hidden from **predators**, they eat tiny sea creatures and spend long hours floating in the warm sun. The heat and food help them grow rapidly.

(Left-hand page, top) *A female loggerhead sea turtle lays her eggs in the hole she has dug high on the beach.* (Left-hand page, bottom) *A close-up of the loggerhead's eggs.* (Above) *The female loggerhead rests on the beach after laying her eggs. (Lynn Stone)*

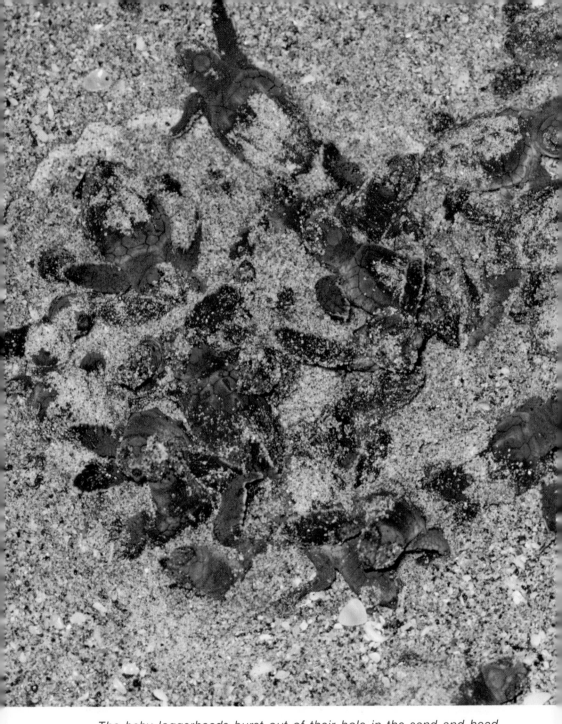

The baby loggerheads burst out of their hole in the sand and head straight for the sea. (Lynn Stone)

One baby loggerhead has just about reached the safety of the sea. Once in the water, it will face still more dangers from predators. (Lynn Stone)

Loggerheads have a lot of growing to do. When they hatch, their shells are just 1-3/4 inches (4-1/2 centimeters) long. By the time they become adults, the shell is more than a yard (about a meter) long. If human babies grew as much, people would be more than thirty-five feet (eleven meters) tall and weigh more than twenty-one tons.

Beach babies leave the shore when they hatch. They return to their sandy birthplaces only when ready to lay their own eggs.

3 Strange Egg Cases

Mermaids' purses; sand collars; sea wash balls: What do these strange names have to do with sea babies?

Each is the name of an egg case for some sea animal. Each provides protection to the growing creature until it is ready to hatch. None looks like any kind of egg you have ever seen before.

Skates

A mermaid's purse is a skate's egg case. The flat, diamond-shaped skate has a long, thin tail and is closely related to the dangerous stingray. As it swims through the water, the skate looks like a huge moth. Its wide, winglike flaps propel it swiftly.

At egg-laying time, a female skate finds a spot on the sea bottom to anchor her eggs. Each egg is in a hard black or greenish-brown case that looks somewhat like a tiny purse with a short strap on each corner. The straps, or horns, on one end anchor the egg case to sand and shell.

Inside, the tiny skate grows like a chicken in an egg. In two weeks it is long and thin like an eel. By seven weeks, the wing flaps have formed, and the tiny embryo begins to look like a skate. Its big black eyes bulge within the egg case. During the next week the wing flaps grow so large that there is no room for them to stretch out. They fold around the tiny creature. At the end of about eight weeks, one end of the case splits open. The little skate swims out, unfolding its wings as it goes. With a final flip of its tail it is free of the case.

Mermaids' purses often wash ashore. The ones you are most likely to find are hard and black. They may be three inches (eight centimeters) long. Some kinds of skates, however, have purses almost a foot (thirty-two centimeters) long.

Sharks

Some sharks also lay their eggs in mermaids' purses. Long straps on the corners anchor the cases to rocks and **corals**. The baby sharks take much longer than skates to develop. In fact, nine months to a year pass before the young emerge. They are strong and healthy, ready to sink their teeth into a tasty fish.

A swell shark rests on the sea bottom. It lays its eggs in hard cases anchored to rocks and corals. About nine months later, strong and healthy young swell sharks emerge from the egg cases. (Robert Commer/EarthViews)

Whelks

Tough, leathery cases protect the eggs of certain sea snails. Each of these snails has its own special kind of egg case.

Large marine snails called whelks form strings of coin-shaped disks, each the size of a nickel, or even as large as a quarter. A tough string holds them together like beads dangling from a necklace.

Buccinum Snails

The small Buccinum snail forms its dime-sized egg cases into a cluster which looks like a big, spongy ball. Long ago, sailors used the clusters as soap and called them sea wash balls. Imagine what it would be like to bathe with a ball of egg cases!

Dogwinkles

The little dogwinkle forms egg cases that look almost like grains of ripe wheat. Each case is attached to a hard surface. Many cases are crowded together in little groups on rocks or shells where they sway with the movement of the tides.

Making the egg cases is a slow job for a female sea snail. Her body secretes the special fluid needed to form the tough covering. It may take several days to complete a string, cluster, or group of egg cases. Into each the snail lays many eggs, but not all will hatch. Some are nurse eggs, placed in the case to feed the tiny snails as they develop.

When the snails hatch, they have miniature shells no bigger than half a grain of rice. They crawl out a hole in the edge of the case and are washed away by the waves. Soon the tiny creatures begin their search for food among the sand and rocks near the shore.

As the snail grows, it secretes a liquid that hardens into shell. The shell grows larger as layers of shell are added to the open end. If the seawater is too hot, too cold, or **polluted**, the shell grows slowly or not at all. When conditions are right, the baby snail adds many tiny layers of shell.

The shell is the snail's skeleton. It is rough on the outside and smooth and shiny inside. To move around, the snail sticks its foot and head out of the shell. The other end of its body is firmly attached inside. If there is danger, the snail hides in its shell and blocks the opening with a "trap door," the **operculum**, on its foot.

The dogwinkle will grow about two inches (five centimeters) long, and the Buccinum snail twice as long. The large whelks can grow as long as a person's foot. Whatever their size as adults, all three begin life as tiny snails in tough egg cases.

Moon Snails

The moon snail builds a collar of sand around its shell. The eggs are laid in a jellylike band that picks up a layer of sand on both sides. As the band wraps around the moon snail's shell, the jelly and sand hard-

en. When the snail moves away, the sand collar stays. The eggs are in little chambers in the sandy band.

Sand collars are often found on mud flats and in shallow bays. They rest on the bottom, undisturbed by gentle waves. After about four months, the jelly softens, and the baby snails leave. The collar is now useless and breaks apart.

Strange egg cases with strange names give some sea creatures a good start in life.

The moon snail lays its eggs in a jellylike band that hardens into a sand collar. This moon snail was observed along the coast of Florida. (Lynn Stone)

# 4 Fathers' Babies

When there is egg watching or egg sitting to be done in the sea, the female usually does it. Sometimes the male shares the job. For several kinds of fish, though, the male takes over completely. The female fish simply lays the eggs, and then swishes merrily away, never to return.

Toadfish

Toadfish fathers guard nests of eggs hidden in old bottles, cans, or shells on the sea bottom. The thick-headed, mud-colored toadfish is a strange-looking creature. As the male hovers over the eggs, he is fearsome. His huge mouth opens wide to snap viciously at any passing sea animal. In this way he keeps the eggs safe until they hatch.

The baby toadfish have the same thick body and huge mouth of the adults, but their tiny size and lighter coloring make them easier to look at. They move away from the nest to hide in any safe crack or

The strange-looking toadfish has a thick body and huge mouth. Toad-fish fathers guard their nests of eggs by opening their mouths wide and snapping viciously at any passing sea animal. (Allan Roberts)

crevice. Here they lurk lazily, watching for tiny creatures to gobble up. As they become too large for one hiding place, they move along the bottom until they find another.

Sea Catfish

Once toadfish hatch, they are on their own, and the father can go about his business as usual. The

male sea catfish is not so fortunate. He not only protects his eggs, but also provides a nursery for the baby
fish—in his mouth!

The female sea catfish drops the marble-sized
eggs in muddy coastal waters and leaves them. If left
alone, the eggs would sink into the mud and smother.
Suddenly the male catfish comes to the rescue. He
scoops the eggs into his mouth and carries them for
two months, bathing them frequently with fresh seawater. A two-foot-long (.6-meter-long) male may have
as many as fifty or sixty marble-sized eggs in his
mouth at one time. But that is the easy part of his job.

When the eggs hatch, the two-inch-long (five-
centimeter long) fish have heavy yolk sacs on their
bellies. Since they cannot swim freely, the catfish
father continues to provide a safe nest. Imagine carrying several dozen wriggling fish in your mouth for a
month!

With its whiskerlike feelers, the sea catfish baby
looks like its parents. It has a stiff spine on top of
its head that will become a dangerous weapon as it
grows. Any angler who catches a sea catfish should
watch out for the spine.

Probably no other baby fish is so carefully cared

The sea catfish has whiskerlike feelers and a stiff spine on top of its head. When the female lays eggs in the sea, the male scoops them up and protects them in its mouth until a month after they have hatched. (Allan Roberts)

for as the sea catfish. Most fish fry, or babies, are left to fend for themselves in a sea full of hungry creatures. But the catfish father does not let his young go until they are several weeks old. By then they are about four inches (ten centimeters) long. The father cannot eat the entire time he is carrying the eggs and fish.

A bright yellow sea horse hovers over a colony of brain coral. This sea horse appears to be a father carrying eggs that were placed in its pouch by the sea horse mother. (Stephen Frink/WaterHouse)

Sea Horses

Sea horses are fascinating creatures. Unlike other fish, they swim upright, with heads up and tails down. They have heads that look like horse's heads. The most curious thing about sea horses, though, is that the fathers have the babies. The mother's only job is to put eggs in a pouch on the belly of the father.

Inside the pouch is a group of tiny compartments

full of blood vessels . An egg settles into each compartment, attaching to the wall. The blood vessels carry oxygen and **nutrients** to the eggs so that they can develop.

Like any pregnant mother, the sea horse father has a fat belly. Depending upon the species, the young are fully developed in from ten to fifty days. Finally the eggs hatch, and the male presses against a rock or hard piece of seaweed to push the tiny babies out into the sea. They shoot out of an opening in the top of the pouch and hide among strands of seaweed.

Two days after the young sea horses leave, the father is ready for more eggs. He may carry eggs as many as eighteen times a year. During the winter months, he rests.

Both young and adult sea horses need the protection of their seaweed homes. Since their tiny fins do not allow them to swim rapidly, their protection comes from being hidden. The seahorses wrap the ends of their tails around pieces of seaweed and hang on. Because their body colors blend with the seaweeds, the 1/4-inch-long (2/3-centimeter-long) babies are nearly hidden in their seaweed homes. If they leave, they soon become food for some larger fish.

Thanks to their fathers, baby toadfish, sea cat-fish, and sea horses get a good start in their struggle to survive in the ocean world.

5 River Babies

Many fish spend a good part of their lives traveling. They travel in search of food and with currents or tides. They travel to stay in cold waters or warm waters. And they travel to spawn.

Shad, Alewife, and Striped Bass

Some fish have regular spawning places where they go to lay their eggs. Shad, alewife, and striped bass are fish that live in the sea. But at spawning time, they travel into freshwater streams and rivers. As they move into the inland waters, their bodies adjust to the absence of salt. They can lay their eggs in the safer river waters where the young will find plenty of food. The young may spend several months as river babies before traveling to the sea.

Salmon

The most spectacular spawning trip made by any fish is that of salmon. Coming from hundreds of miles out in the sea, they buck currents and waves to find the mouth of the river where they were born. For a while they swim about near the river mouth to get used to the fresher waters before starting upstream.

Once in the rivers, the salmon may travel more than 1000 miles to reach the spawning ground of their choice. All their energy is concentrated on the trip. They do not eat. They do not turn back. They swim against the swift current that carries the river water to the sea, and struggle through the surging white water of huge rapids. They leap as high as twelve feet (nearly four meters) into the air, flinging themselves over waterfalls. Their bodies become bruised and cut from hitting rocks. Exhausted and sore, they finally reach quiet pools where they settle down.

Adult salmon may weigh from five pounds (more than two kilograms) to as much as one hundred pounds (forty-five kilograms). They spend several months in fresh water, fed only by the fat that had built up in their bodies in the sea. When frosty fall and winter nights turn the water cold, spawning takes place.

Female salmon, called hen fish, search the gravel bottom of a stream for the best spawning places. They

On its way to spawn, an Alaskan salmon leaps out of the water in an effort to fling itself over a waterfall. (G. Hahnel/U.S. Fish and Wildlife Service)

push and shove, fighting for their spots. But their quarrels are mild compared to the fights of the males, or cock fish. Cocks charge at each other like boxers in a ring. The strongest butt others with their powerful heads, driving off the weaker fish.

At last, a hen and a cock settle down to the serious business of nesting. First the hen swishes her tail against the gravel, scooping out a shallow hole. Settling into the hole, she lays several thousand eggs. Immediately the cock covers the eggs with his milt, or sperm, and then swims away to another nest. The hen covers the nest with gravel, and then she leaves, too. Pacific salmon die once they have spawned, but many Atlantic salmon swim back out to sea. They will return to spawn another year.

In spring the eggs hatch. At first the tiny fish are held to the bottom by the weight of the yolk sac on their bellies. Their black eyes bulge on tiny transparent bodies. The salmon babies look much like any other freshly hatched fish. After several weeks in the gravel, the babies have used up their yolk sacs. They are now about an inch (almost three centimeters) long and ready to swim away.

For several years the young salmon live in the

river, feeding on insects and worms. When the river babies reach about six inches (fifteen centimeters) in length, they turn silver and head for the sea. Once in the ocean, they gather together in schools. Then off they go, hundreds of miles away from shore. When they return, they will be big, fat, and ready to build their own nests.

Eels

Snakelike eels also travel great distances to spawn, but they go in the opposite direction of salmon. From the rivers of Europe and America, adult eels swim into the sea. They find their way to a special spawning area in deep waters more than 1,000 miles (1,600 kilometers) from their homes. The females lay about ten million eggs each, and the males shed their sperm. Then the adults die, leaving the babies to carry on into the next generation.

Eel larvae look like tiny flat fish. They are thin as wafers and so transparent that you can see their insides. As soon as the larvae hatch, the tiny eels begin their journey toward the rivers. The trip may take a year or more, for they have more than 1,000 miles (1,600 kilometers) to go.

By the time they arrive, their bodies have changed. The eels are longer and rounder and begin to develop the snakelike look of the adults. Their skin begins to turn brown. They become river babies, growing and fattening as they mature into adults. Years later, like their parents, they move back into the sea to spawn.

How do salmon and eels find their way over hundreds of miles to special spots to spawn? How do river babies find their way into or out of rivers? How do they know when and where to go? No one knows the answers to these questions. Scientists have proposed theories to explain the behavior of salmon and eels, but they do not know for sure. So far, the travels of river babies and their parents remain mysteries. Perhaps someday they will be solved.

6 Mammal Babies

Seals, dolphins, and whales are **mammals**, or warm-blooded animals. Dogs, cats, horses, and people are mammals, too. Like land mammals, sea mammals are born alive, rather than hatching from eggs, and they nurse on their mother's milk. Since they have lungs to breathe the air, they must come to the surface of the water to breathe.

Harp Seals

If a contest were held to choose the cutest sea baby, the harp seal would win first prize. This roly-poly, snow white creature lies on the ice and stares at the world through big, black eyes. A black patch of fur marks its nose and mouth. Soft white fur covers its round little body and the flippers it has instead of arms and legs.

Thousands of harp seal cows gather on drifting pack ice in Arctic regions. Each has one **pup**. For the first week, the mother does not leave the side of her

Shortly after giving birth, a harp seal mother rests on the Arctic ice next to her helpless pup. For many years hunters came to the Arctic pack ice to kill harp seal babies for their soft white fur. Now governments have taken some actions to protect the babies. (David Rinehart/Greenpeace)

helpless pup. She feeds it her extra rich milk so that it will grow a thick layer of blubber or fat to protect it from the cold. At birth the pup weighs about fifteen pounds (about seven kilograms). After three weeks it has reached one hundred pounds (forty-five kilograms) and looks as if it has swallowed a balloon.

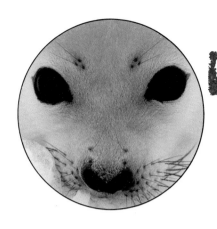

A close-up of the face of a harp seal baby on the Arctic ice. (David Rinehart/Greenpeace)

Harp seal cows begin leaving the pups for short periods during their second week of life. What a commotion that causes! The pups cry as long as their mothers are gone. Ten thousand babies crying at once make the seal nursery a very noisy place.

The cows always return to their own pups, and they will nurse no other. Sometimes, however, a pup chooses the wrong mother. When that happens, the cow sends it away with a slap of a flipper. For three weeks the cows feed and care for their pups, and then the mother leaves the pup alone.

For a week or so, the pup goes without food while it begins to shed its fluffy white coat. A shorter gray fur grows underneath. Now the pup is ready to enter the water and search for small sea creatures for food. During the next two years its fur coat becomes a darker gray, with a black patch covering its head and middle of its back.

At first the young seals stay by themselves while they swim and feed near the ice. Later they follow the adults as they move north.

Seals come ashore to rest and to have their pups. Otherwise they live in the sea because their bodies are adapted for moving swiftly through the water. In the sea, front flippers form powerful paddles, and back flippers serve to guide them. On land, the creatures move slowly and awkwardly, flopping forward with their flippers.

Sea Lions

Different species of seals live in different parts of the world. The ones we are most familiar with are the California sea lions—the performing seals. They are popular in circus and zoo acts because of their amazing ability to do a number of tricks.

Sea lions live in warmer areas than their harp seal cousins. The pups can swim freely by the time they are two weeks old, but they remain close to their mothers for five or six months. During this time they feed on the mother's milk and begin to eat some small fish.

The bull, or father, is the mate for about forty sea lion cows which he keeps together and protects until their pups are old enough to live by themselves. He watches over the cows and pups and threatens any enemy that appears. A male sea lion can rear up on its hind flippers and stand almost six feet (nearly two meters) tall. His 600-pound (273-kilogram) body and

Young California sea lions play in shallow waters near the U.S. Pacific coast. (Marty Snyderman/WaterHouse)

loud roar are enough to frighten almost any approaching animal. If a pup goes into the water before it can swim, the bull gets very upset. His loud, hoarse bark alerts the mother to go to the rescue of the pup.

Young sea lions are playful creatures. They dive and somersault in the water, flip up onto the shore, and then flop back into the sea. They chase each other in water games and bark joyfully as they play.

The furry seals are not hard to identify as mammals. Other mammals in the sea, however, can be mistaken for fish.

Dolphins and whales, despite their appearance, are mammals. Blowholes on top of their heads serve as nostrils for breathing air. These creatures will drown if they cannot reach the surface to breathe. Instead of fur, a thick layer of blubber keeps their bodies warm. Like most mammals, dolphins and whales are intelligent creatures and take good care of their young.

Dolphins

A baby dolphin is born tail first. Its tail fins are soft and folded inward, but open rapidly. At once the newborn creature flutters its tail and heads for the surface to breathe. The mother dolphin gently helps with a nudge of her nose. The female dolphins in the herd circle close by to protect the newborn **calf** and its mother. Often one special female is a mother's helper and stays close by at all times.

The baby dolphin is a small version of its mother. Compared to a human baby, it is large—at least three feet (nearly one meter) long and weighing about twenty-four pounds (almost eleven kilograms). It soon finds its mother's milk. Instead of having to suck like a puppy or kitten does, the baby dolphin squeezes the mother's teat with its tongue. A huge gulp of milk squirts into its mouth. With a quick swallow, the calf rises to the surface to breathe, and then comes back for another squirt.

Like seal milk, dolphin milk is extremely rich in nutrients. Since mammals must grow quickly, they need the layer of fat the milk helps them develop. Baby dolphins like nothing better than the fishy smelling, oily tasting milk that is their first food.

When not eating, the baby dolphin swims close to the lower half of the mother's body. Its swimming is a bit wobbly at first. It must flutter its tail rapidly to keep up with the mother. For the first three months of

A Hawaiian spinner dolphin leaps out of the sea. All dolphins are active, playful creatures, and the young are the most playful of all. (Randall S. Wells/EarthViews)

the baby's life, the dolphin mother watches it closely, never letting it stray more than ten feet (three meters) away. The two often go up to breathe together, the infant bobbing and splashing, and the mother surfacing in a smooth roll.

By the second week or so of its life, the dolphin calf begins to move away from its safe spot to play around the mother's head. It rubs and nuzzles like a child who wants a little attention.

After three months, the baby begins to swim farther away. Though it will continue to nurse for a year and a half, it will also start eating small fish. Throughout this time, the dolphin mother will always be nearby. In case of danger, the entire herd will bunch together to protect the mothers and young in the middle.

All dolphins are active, playful creatures, and the young are the most playful of all. They chase each other and tease other animals such as turtles or large fish. They invent active games, twisting and turning in the water and popping up into the air. At times they annoy the mothers and other adults, just as human children do. Dolphin mothers have much patience, though. While they may push the overactive young away, they never get rough with them.

Dolphins have a language of their own that babies hear from birth. For the first few days the mother whistles constantly. The calf learns to recognize the sound, and the mother also recognizes the little whistles and squeaks of her own calf.

Whales

The life of baby whales is much like that of baby dolphins. Whale babies, however, are much larger. The biggest baby in the world is the baby blue whale. It may be twenty-three feet (seven meters) long and weigh two and a half tons at birth—larger than a car.

The adult blue whale is the largest animal that has ever lived. It may grow as long as two buses and weigh more than twenty-five elephants. Even a dinosaur—if one were still living—would look small beside a full grown blue whale.

The baby blue whale drinks a half ton of milk a day, and each day it gains more than 200 pounds (91 kilograms). By the time it is a year old, it is fifty feet (about fifteen meters) long. By age two, it is fully grown.

The young blue whale stops nursing at six

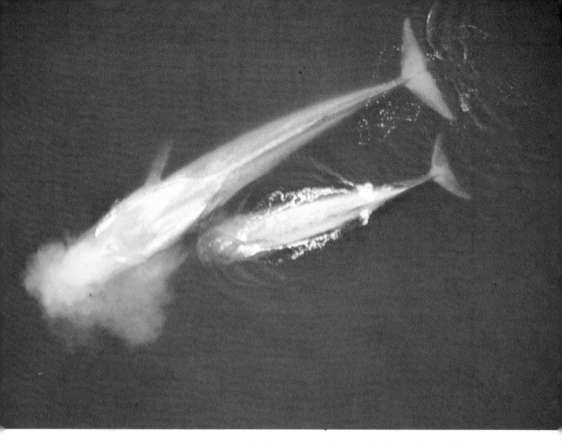

A baby blue whale swims through the ocean alongside its mother. The adult blue whale is the largest animal that has ever lived. (Stan Minasian/ EarthViews)

months of age and is ready to live on its own. This huge mammal eats tiny sea creatures that it strains out of the water. It is a gentle giant.

Of all parents in the ocean, the sea mammals give their babies the best care. The mammals have only a small number of babies compared to other sea animals. Each mammal baby, though, has a much better chance to grow to adulthood.

7 Sea Nurseries

Along the coastlines, rivers flow into the sea. Bays, bayous, and inlets cut into the land. Fresh water from the rivers and salt water from the sea mix together. Where the full force of ocean waves is blocked by fingers of land and shallow banks, the partly enclosed bodies of water are known as **estuaries**. They are the nurseries of the sea.

A Home for Sea Life

Into these protected areas, fish come to lay their eggs, or their young come to mature. Oysters, clams, and crabs spend their lives in estuaries. So important are the estuaries to life in the sea that we would have very little seafood without them. More than three-fourths of the creatures used as seafood on the east coast and half on the west coast spend some part of their lives in estuaries.

Salt marshes cover much of the land around estuaries. Here tough strands of cordgrass reach higher

A heron stands in the shallow waters of an estuary at dawn. (Lynn Stone)

than a person's waist. Their matted roots help filter out chemical poisons that wash from the cities and farms into the sea.

Strands of cordgrass break off and fall into the marsh where they begin to decay. The small pieces wash into the estuaries along with decaying bits of leaves from trees and other plants. Together, these decaying bits of plants form a substance called **detritus**. Small **algae** or sea plants mix with detritus in a kind of sea vegetable soup. This soup is the basic food for fish, shrimp, crabs, and clams. These, in turn, become food for larger fish and for birds.

Microscopic plankton—tiny plants and animals—float in the estuaries. They add to the food supply of the larger sea creatures.

Seaweeds and grasses cover many underwater areas. In these watery jungles, tiny animals find safe homes. Beneath the sand and mud, many kinds of clams and marine worms find shelter. Tiny holes in the sand mark their homes, and sometimes a squirt of water bursts out from one of these holes.

Mud flats may hide many creatures, too. On a quiet day you can sometimes hear the crackling sounds of hidden animals coming from beneath the flats' soft surfaces. Even in the mud, life flourishes.

The sea life in an estuary makes it a busy place. Grouped together in schools, tiny fish dart through the waters. They may burst to the surface with a splash, all moving at once. Baby shrimp huddle around rocks and weeds. Crabs, snails, and starfish wander across the bottom, leaving tiny trails as they go.

Creatures have much growing to do in these protected sea nurseries. They eat and are eaten, because every creature living there is food for another. Still, tiny creatures have a better chance for survival in estuaries than in the open sea. Food is plentiful. The shallow waters and seaweeds provide hiding places from predators. And many larger fish cannot enter the area because the water is not salty enough for them.

Threatened Estuaries

Without estuaries, there would be no sea nurseries for many creatures. Without the nurseries, the young could not survive, and their species would become **extinct**. Each species is food for another. Without that food, other species would become extinct, too.

The sea is huge, covering nearly three-fourths of the earth's surface. It has more living creatures and more plants than the land. Yet life in this vast ocean is greatly affected by what happens on the land. **Pollution** and destruction of estuaries can destroy life in the open sea. Fish far out in the ocean cannot survive if the nurseries for their young are gone, or if the fish they feed on are gone.

Today, for several reasons, our estuaries are in trouble. Since people like to live by the sea, marshes are covered over with dirt so that homes can be built. Sewers serving homes empty waste into the estuaries. Rain washes fertilizers and **insecticides** from lawns and farms into rivers and into the sea. Huge industries build factories by the sea, fill the marshlands, and dump wastes into the waters. Shopping centers and roads cover areas where marsh grasses once grew.

Sea nurseries are disappearing in many places. In others the waters have become so poisoned that few creatures can live and grow. Anglers report that there are not as many fish as there used to be in most estuaries. In many areas catches of shrimp and crabs are reduced from their former levels, and shellfish are in shorter supply. Yet, throughout the world, there are

This housing development was built over shallow waters along the Florida coast.

more people than ever who need the food from the sea.

Sea nurseries can be saved if people act now to preserve them. Remaining estuaries and marshes can be left undisturbed. Marsh grasses and seaweeds can be replanted where they have died. People living near rivers and bays can be careful with fertilizers and insecticides so that they don't wash into the sea. Human and industrial wastes can be treated and used or stored on land. If we take care of our estuaries now, there will always be enough nurseries for the babies of the sea.

Appendix A:
Learning More About Sea Life

The following activities will help you learn more about sea life. Choose one or more to begin working on today.

1. Begin a sea life scrapbook. Look for articles and pictures of sea life in newspapers and magazines. Get permission to cut them out and paste them in your scrapbook. Draw your own pictures or take photographs if you visit a seashore, zoo, or aquarium that has examples of sea life. For information from books, make a copy of a page or two on a copy machine, or write the information in your own words. You may place a thin piece of paper over interesting pictures and trace them for your scrapbook if you are careful not to mark the book. (Of course, you would never cut anything out of a book!)

2. Begin a sea life collection. Seashells, dried starfish or seahorses, and crab claws and shells are some of the things you can include in it. Try, in particular, to get some egg cases, such as those from whelks or skates. Also, try to include several different sizes of each example of sea life. Boxes of various sizes, such as gift boxes and shoe boxes, can be used to hold your collection. Separate the items with cardboard dividers, or glue each example to the box. Label each item with its name, and the date and place found. You may have to make a trip to the library to learn the names of some of your sea life specimens. You can find your own items, ask friends to send them to you, or purchase them.

Try to learn more about each item in your collection. If an egg case, what animal did it come from? Is there a hole or split where the babies left it? If you have more than one size of a creature or its shell, can you see any difference in the shape or color of the smallest and the largest? Add any interesting facts or observations to the label or to a notecard in your collection box.

3. Visit an estuary area, such as a bay, marsh, bayou, or river mouth. Sit quietly on a dock, sea wall, rock, or shore. What sea animals do you see? How large are they? What are they doing? Look particularly around dock pilings and grassy or seaweed-filled areas. Are there tiny fish swimming around or other tiny creatures such as crabs or shrimp? Make a list of all the creatures you see. How many are sea babies?

4. Compare sizes to gain an understanding of the widely different sizes of sea creatures. First, make a tiny dot with a pencil on a piece of paper. Hold the dot beside a large car. The dot is larger than the smallest sea baby. The car is smaller than the largest sea baby. What baby is that? Hold a soup spoon beside the tire of a large car. The bowl of the spoon is about the size of a baby turtle's shell; the tire the size of its mother's shell. How much must the baby grow to become an adult? How big were you as a baby? How much must you grow to be as large as your parents?

Appendix B:
Scientific Names
for Sea Animals

Sea creatures, like all living things, have two kinds of names. The first is their *common name*, a name in the everyday language of an area where they are found. An animal often has a number of different common names in different languages. Also, several different animals may be known by the same common name.

The second kind of name is their *scientific name*. This is a Latin name assigned by scientists to identify an animal all over the world for other scientists. The scientific name is usually made up of two words. The first identifies a genus, or group, of similar animals (or plants), and the second identifies the species, or kind, of animal in the group. Sometimes, as scientists learn more about an animal, they may decide it belongs to a different group. The scientific name is then changed so that all scientists can recognize it and know exactly what animal it refers to.

If you want to learn more about the creatures in this book, the list of scientific names that follows will be useful to you. A typical species has been identified for each type of animal mentioned in the book. There may be many other species in the same group.

Chapter	Common Name	Scientific Name
1.	Eastern Oyster	*Crassostrea virginica*
	Native Pacific Oyster	*Ostrea lurida*
	Red Abalone	*Haliotis rufescens*
	Pink Shrimp	*Panaeus duorarum*
	Blue Crab	*Callinectes sapidus*
2.	Horseshoe Crab	*Limulus polyphemus*
	Blue Mussel	*Mytilus edulis*
	Grunion	*Leuresthes tenuis*
	Loggerhead Turtle	*Caretto caretta*
3.	Skate	*Raja erinacea*
	Swell Shark	*Cephaloscyllium ventriosum*
	Channeled Whelk	*Busycon canaliculatum*
	Buccinum Snail	*Buccinum undatum*
	Dogwinkle	*Thais lapillus*
	Moon Snail	*Lunatia heros*

Chapter	Common Name	Scientific Name
4.	Toadfish	*Opsanus beta*
	Sea Catfish	*Galeichthys felis*
	Atlantic Sea Horse	*Hippocampus hudsonius*
5.	Shad	*Alosa sapidissima*
	Alewife	*Alosa pseudoharengus*
	Striped Bass	*Roccus saxatilis*
	Pink Salmon	*Oncorhynchus gorbusche*
	American Eel	*Anguilla rostrata*
6.	Harp Seal	*Pusa groenlandica*
	California Sea Lion	*Zalophus californianus*
	Hawaiian Spinner Dolphin	*Stenella longirostris*
	Blue Whale	*Balaenoptera musculus*

 Glossary

algae (AL-jee)—any of a group of mainly aquatic plants, such as seaweed, pond scums, and stonewort, often masked by a brown or red pigment

calf—used here to mean a baby whale or dolphin

cilia (SIL-ee-uh)—used here to describe tiny, hairlike projections that serve as paddles on a baby oyster to propel it through the water

corals—colonies of sea animals, called polyps, that form hard, rocklike skeletons on the outside of their bodies

crevice (KREV-ihs)—a narrow opening resulting from a split or crack

detritus (dih-TRY-tuhs)—decaying bits of cordgrass and leaves that mix with small algae or sea plants in a "soup" that is the basic food for fish, shrimp, crabs, and clams

egg—a round or oval body from a female creature; it contains a yolk and the seed or germ cell of a new creature

embryo (EM-bree-oh)—the first stages of life within a fertilized egg

estuaries (ES-chuh-wair-eez)—partly enclosed bodies of water where fresh water from rivers and streams and salt water from the sea meet and mix

extinct (ek-STINKT)—no longer living anywhere on earth

fertilization (fur-tuh-luh-ZAY-shuhn)—the combining of a sperm and egg to begin the process that gives life to a new creature

fry—baby fish

insecticide (in-SEK-tuh-side)—an agent (usually a chemical) that destroys insects

larva (plural—larvae [LAHR-vee])—an animal baby or early form of an animal that must change its form before taking on the characteristics of an adult

mammals—warm-blooded animals that nurse their young on milk from their bodies and have skin usually covered with hair

marine biologists—scientists who study the animals and plants of the sea

mermaid's purse—a name given to the egg case of skates and some sharks

microscope—an instrument that magnifies objects too small to be seen clearly with the naked eye

microscopic (my-kro-SCOP-ik)—extremely small in size; an object that can be seen only with a microscope

milt (MIHLT)—the sperm of male fish

molt (MOHLT)—to cast off or shed the outer covering; certain sea creatures molt as they grow

nutrients (NYU-tree-ents)—substances that promote the growth of living things

operculum (oh-PURR-kyu-luhm)—the "trap door" that a marine snail uses to block the opening of its shell when threatened

predator (PREHD-uh-tuhr)—an animal that kills and eats another animal

pup—used here to mean a baby seal

plankton—tiny plants and animals that float in the sea; many are microscopic

pollute—to make foul or unclean; human and industrial wastes have polluted many estuaries

pollution—any substance that makes water, land, or air dirty or impure

sand collar—a name given to the egg case of a moon snail

school—used here to mean a large number of fish swimming together

seaquarium (see-KWAIR-ee-uhm)—a sea aquarium, or huge tank filled with seawater in which sea animals and plants can be viewed and studied

sea wash balls—an old sailors' term given to the egg cases of the Buccinum snail because they were used in place of soap

secrete (sih-KREET)—to form and give off a substance

shellfish—sea animals that have shells, such as clams and snails

spat—baby oyster

spawn—to produce eggs and sperm; salmon and seals may travel long distances to spawn

species (SPEE-sheez)—distinct kinds of individual plants or animals that have common characteristics and share a common name

sperm—the seed or germ cell from a male

tentacles—armlike extensions on the body of a sea animal; used for moving, feeling, or grasping

transparent—made of such material that objects can be seen from the other side; see-through

trillion—a thousand billion; written as 1,000,000,000,000

zoea (zoh-EE-uh)—a crab larva

Selected Bibliography

Books

Brown, Ann Ensign. *Wonders of Sea Horses*. New York: Dodd, Mead, 1979.

Burton, Maurice, and Burton, Robert, eds. *The International Wildlife Encyclopedia*. New York: Marshall Cavendish, 1969.

Bustard, Robert. *Sea Turtles, Their Natural History and Conservation*. London: William Collins, 1972.

Carson, Rachel. *Edge of the Sea*. New York: Houghton Mifflin, 1955.

Jenkins, Marie M. *The Curious Mollusks*. New York: Holiday House, 1972.

Martin, Richard Mark. *Mammals of the Oceans*. New York: Putnam's, 1977.

Moorcraft, Colin. *Must The Seas Die?* Boston: Gambit, 1973.

Soule, Gardiner. *Remarkable Creatures of the Seas*. New York: Putnam's, 1975.

Teal, John and Mildred. *Life and Death of the Salt Marsh*. Boston: Little, Brown, 1969.

Vevers, Gwynne. *Fishes*. New York: McGraw-Hill, 1976.

Articles

Clark, Eugenie. "Sharks, Magnificent and Misunderstood." *National Geographic*, August 1981, pp. 138-186.

Fisher, Allan C. Jr. "My Chesapeake—Queen of Bays." *National Geographic*, October 1980, pp. 428-467.

Hitchcock, Stephen W. "Can We Save Our Salt Marshes?" *National Geographic*, June 1972, pp. 729-765.

Idyll, Clarence P. "Grunion, The Fish That Spawns on Land." *National Geographic*, May 1969, pp. 714-723.

———. "Shrimp Nursery: Science Explores New Ways to Farm the Sea." *National Geographic*, May 1965, pp. 635-659.

Lavigne, David M. "Life or Death for the Harp Seal." *National Geographic*, January 1976, pp. 129-142.

Lee, Art. "Atlantic Salmon, The 'Leaper' Struggles to Survive." *National Geographic*, November 1981, pp. 600-614.

Libby, Ernest L. "Miracle of the Mermaid's Purse." *National Geographic*, September 1959, pp.412-420.

Rudloe, Anne and Jack. "The Changeless Horseshoe Crab." *National Geographic*, April 1981, 562-572.

 Index

The photographs are reproduced through the courtesy of Earth-Views and the Marine Mammal Fund (Robert Commer, Jacki Kilbride, Stan Minasian, and Randall S. Wells, photographers); Greenpeace (David Rinehart, photographer); Allan Roberts; James Rowan; Lynn Stone; the U.S. Fish and Wildlife Service (G. Hahnel, photographer); and WaterHouse (Stephen Frink and Marty Snyderman, photographers). Cover: A newly born harp seal pup lays on the Arctic pack ice.

About the Author

Jean Sibbald's interest in sea life started in childhood when, as the daughter of a marine biologist, she grew up on a marine biological station. Although her career has taken other directions since then, she was and is an avid amateur conchologist.

Sea Babies, says the author, "introduces young readers to the strangest babies in the world—the babies of sea creatures. In vivid detail, the book describes babies hatched by the millions and scattered in the sea to fend for themselves. It describes others that are carefully nurtured, or are protected in unusual ways. How they begin, how they grow, how they look—these are just some of the things readers will learn about in Sea Babies."

Ms. Sibbald's educational background includes an undergraduate major in biology and a bachelor's and master's degree in speech communication. Currently she is a district staff development and training manager for the Florida Department of Health and Rehabilitative Services. The mother of two children, she lives in Tampa, Florida.